e-mail
wizard

10 9 8 7 6 5 4 3 2 1

First published in the UK in 2001 by Big Fish.
Distributed by Sterling Publishing Company Inc.,
387, Park Avenue South, New York, N.Y. 100016.
Distributed in Canada by Sterling Publishing,
c/o Canadian Manda group, One Atlantic Avenue,
Suite 105, Toronto, Ontario, Canada M6K 3E7.

ISBN 0-8069-7515-6

Printed in China

Project Management: Honor Head
Project Editor: Kate Phelps
Designer: Louise Morley
Illustrator: Debi Ani

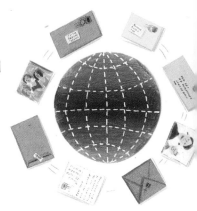

e-mail wizard

Anne Rooney
Illustrated by Debi Ani

CONTENTS

BETTER THAN A LETTER

E-mail is a quick, cheap and fun way to keep in touch with your friends. Even a simple e-mail is better than a letter and once you get to be an e-mail whizz you can really show off.

You can learn

- what e-mail is
- what you need to get started

What's it all about?

E-mail means 'electronic mail'. It started in the 1960s when people first had the idea of joining computers together so that they could send messages and information between them. To start with it was rather primitive and was only used by a few eggheads in lab-coats or cardigans. But since the World Wide Web took off in the 1990s, e-mail has come to everyone and is one of our most popular ways of keeping in touch.

- the postage stamp was invented in 1837; we now send 1.200 billion letters a day around the world!

- the phone was invented in 1876; there are now about 800 million phone lines around the world.

- the first program to send and read e-mail was written in 1971; by the end of 2001 there will be a billion e-mail accounts around the world — more than TVs or phone lines!

Snail-mail

When you send a letter by snail-mail, you have to write it or print it out on paper, put it in an envelope, write the address on the outside, stick a stamp on it and put it in the mail box. And then the letter has to wait for the mailman or mailwoman to pick it up and take it to a sorting office where it's put in the right sack for the town it's going to. It's then moved by road or rail, sorted again when it gets there and taken by bicycle or on foot to the right house. It's all a bit of a hassle, but quite good value at about 3 cents per day.

In a second

When you send an e-mail, you type in your message and the e-mail address of the person you want to send it to and click the 'Send' button. (Your message is its own envelope — the e-mail address is at the top and that's the bit the computers read — and it needs no stamp.) Your computer sends it down the phone line (that's like putting it in the mail box) and other computers send it along the quickest route (they replace the sorting office, the vans and trains and the postal workers). And instead of days, it takes seconds or minutes. All of which is pretty good value for a couple of pennies or nothing at all!

What do you need?

You'll need a computer with an Internet connection and an e-mail account. Probably. You can also use a set-top cable TV box or some types of phone. But we'll stick to computers. This is what you'll need:

A modem: you don't need the latest model of computer, but you need one with a modem. This is a bit of equipment that connects your computer to the phone line. It changes information from your computer to a form that can be carried along the phone lines. The modem might be a box that sits on the desk or it might be a card inside your computer.

If you don't have a modem already, find out all you can about your computer before you go out to buy one so that you get the right one.

A phone socket: your modem needs to be plugged into a phone socket when you want to go on the Internet to send or pick up your e-mail. Your modem doesn't need to be plugged in when you aren't using the Internet. But it doesn't matter if you leave it plugged in. It won't stop you getting phone calls and it won't cost anything except when you're actually on-line.

> You're 'on-line' when you're connected to the Internet, 'off-line' the rest of the time.

An ISP account: to use the Internet, you need an account with an Internet Service Provider (or ISP). This is a company that gets you on to the Internet. Your computer uses the modem and phone line to connect to the ISP's computer. Their computer acts as your way in to the Internet. All your e-mail will go through your ISP's computer on its way to and from yours.

You can find CD-ROMs from ISPs in computer magazines and in lots of stores like supermarkets. The CD installs the software you need to get to the ISP's computer and use the Internet. Make sure you get PC software if you have a PC or Mac software if you have a Mac.

An e-mail account: you need an account with an e-mail service provider. This may be your ISP or you can set up a web-based e-mail account. There are lots of websites you can do this from and it's free. There is more about setting up an e-mail account in 'On your account' on page 12.

E-mail software: you might want to use special e-mail software, but you don't have to. If you want to write and read your e-mail on a web page, fine — you don't need any extra software besides the web browser you use to look at the web page. But if you want to be able to keep your e-mail on your own computer and write and read it off-line, you'll need some e-mail software. You may well have Outlook Express already, as it comes free with many new computers.

If you don't already have some e-mail software, start off by using e-mail on the World Wide Web.

ON YOUR ACCOUNT

You can't get letters in the mail if you don't have somewhere people can send them to, and you can't get e-mail if you don't have an e-mail address. So first things first — get your address sorted.

You can learn

- to work with e-mail on-line and off-line
- how to set up a private e-mail account of your own

There are two ways of working with e-mail on your computer.

E-mail software: you can use an e-mail program that lets you write and read your e-mail when you are not connected to the Internet. This might be Outlook, Outlook Express, Eudora or QuickMail — or something else; there are lots. You only need to connect to the Internet when you want to send or pick up your mail. All your messages are kept on the hard disk of your own computer. (And you can copy them off and keep them on zip disks, writable CDs or floppy disks if you run out of room.)

E-mail from the web: you can send and read all your e-mail from a web page. You need to be connected to the Internet all the time you are using your e-mail, so this costs a bit more unless your Internet calls are free. Your messages are all kept on a server (a fast computer with lots of disk space) owned by your e-mail service provider. You can't keep all your messages for ever as there will be a limit to the amount of disk space you are allowed to use on the server. They might delete your older messages after a certain time, too. (You can copy individual messages on to your own computer if you really want to keep them.)

If you've got e-mail software, you can probably set it up to work with your web e-mail account. There might be instructions on the web page for the e-mail, or look in the help for your e-mail program.

Now work out what to do next:

Does your computer already have an e-mail account on it?

Yes → Is it just yours, or shared with other people? → Just yours → Good – you don't need to do anything!

Shared

No → Start your own e-mail account

Even if there's already an e-mail account for the computer you're using, if it's not yours alone it's worth setting up a private e-mail account that's just for you. That way, you can keep prying brothers and sisters and curious parents away from your juicy secrets.

Open an account

There are lots of websites and businesses that will be happy to give you an e-mail account. If you haven't got Internet access at all yet, you can get a CD-ROM from an Internet Service Provider that will get you on the Web and probably give you an e-mail account at the same time. You can get CDs that get you on to the Internet from computer magazines or shops — many book shops and supermarkets give them away free.

Something for nothing?

Why might someone give away free e-mail accounts? Well, you'll find there are lots of advertisements on the web pages you use to look at and send your e-mail. The service sells advertising space for more money if more people are thought to be looking at their page. They give you an e-mail account so that you are looking at their page and that way they can get money from advertisers — but of course you don't have to read the advertisements or buy the things they advertise!

If you're already on the Net, go to **http://www.bigfishonline.co.uk /whizzkids** to find a list of web pages from which you can set up an e-mail account. There are some especially for kids, and some for just about anyone. It's best to use one intended for kids as there won't be advertisements for unsuitable or boring things on it.

If you have a web e-mail account, you can pick up and send your e-mail from anywhere that you can get to a computer on the Internet — at school, in a library, at a friend's house or even in a cyber café on vacation!

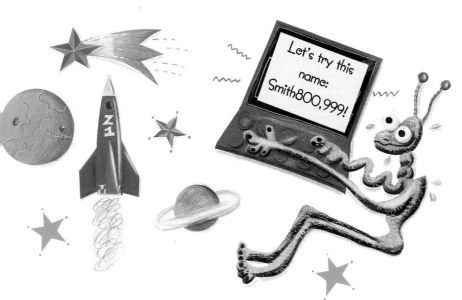

What's in a name?

When you set up an e-mail account, you will need to think
of a name and a password. Your e-mail address will be
made up from the name you pick. You probably won't be
able to use just your first name, unless it's very unusual,
as these will have gone already. But you may be able to
use your nickname, or your name with a number, or more
than one of your names. You might be able to put dots
between the letters of your name, or you can use a dash
(–) or underscore (_). Your e-mail address will then have
an @ ('at') symbol and the name of the e-mail provider.
So it could be something like this:

woppa@mye-mail.com

lauren-heloise@mye-mail.com

gabriella17@mye-mail.com

What's the password?

You will also need a password. This is a secret word that you use to prove that you are really you! When you check in to look at your e-mail, you will need to give the name and password. If they don't match, you won't get to look at your messages. It's a way of stopping other people snooping around your e-mail and sending out messages as though they were from you. (This could be bad — how would you feel if your brother sent a message to your mom saying you'd decided you didn't want any birthday presents?)

Give me a clue

Some services let you set a 'hint question'. This is a question they will ask you if you can't remember your password. Get the question right and you're in. So try not to use a hint question anyone else can answer.

Your password should be something that you can remember but other people can't guess. So don't use your pet's name or your birthday. And don't write the password on a post-it note stuck to the computer!

18

In the register

You will probably have to give a few personal details when you register for a new e-mail address. You should give your real name, as this will probably be shown on your messages and it might be confusing if you used a false name. But you don't have to give your real address.

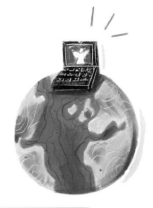

Help box

The details you give might be used for sending you advertising — look for a box on the form that you can tick to say you don't want advertising if this bothers you, though there isn't always one there.

When you've filled in the form on screen, you'll need to send it — that's your first e-mail — and wait for the service to register you. It should take a few minutes, but at the most you should be able to use your e-mail the next day.

So start thinking of people to mail!

YOUR FIRST E-MAIL

You should be ready and raring to go by now. Start with something simple, but soon you'll be sending all kinds of things to all your friends and family.

You can learn ...

- about the parts of an e-mail message: what you write and where
- how to send your first message
- how to look at the reply

New mail

Click on a 'New message' button, icon or similar to write an e-mail. A box will appear with an e-mail message. It has lots of spaces to fill in. On page 21 there is a typical e-mail message so you can see what goes where.

Lots of spaces

In the first space, you type the e-mail address of the person you are sending the message to. Make sure you get it right because your message won't get there if you make any mistakes. If you want to send the message to more than one person, you can add more e-mail addresses here.

Sometimes you put commas between them, like this:
emma_knowles@mye-mail.com, luki@luki2000.com

Sometimes you put semicolons, like this:
emma_knowles@mye mail.com; luki@luki2000.com

You'll need to find out which your program uses.
It's a good idea to put something in the 'subject'
space to tell people what the message is about.

What's in a message

Here's a typical e-mail:

**Spaces for your e-mail address and the e-mail address
of the person you're writing to (if you have stored their
address it might show their name – also called an alias).**

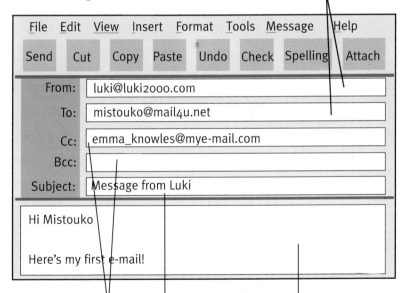

| File | Edit | View | Insert | Format | Tools | Message | Help |

| Send | Cut | Copy | Paste | Undo | Check | Spelling | Attach |

From:	luki@luki2000.com
To:	mistouko@mail4u.net
Cc:	emma_knowles@mye-mail.com
Bcc:	
Subject:	Message from Luki

Hi Mistouko

Here's my first e-mail!

**Spaces for more
addresses so that you
can send copies to
other people (see
pages 22 and 23).**

**A space for you to
put the subject of
the e-mail.**

**A big space for
the main part of
the message.**

Copy me in

If you just want to let someone else know what you've said in a message, you can put their e-mail address in the 'Cc' or 'Copy to' space. So you might e-mail three friends to invite them to lunch, but copy it to your mom to let her know. It's rude to send the message to only one friend and copy it to the other two — they might feel they aren't as important as the 'To' person!

If you have trouble working out whether to include someone in the 'To' space or copy the message to them, think what you would say if you were phoning them. Would you say 'I told Simon...' or would you just say it? 'Copy to' is like saying 'I told him...'.

To:	santa@ntlworld.com
Cc:	
Bcc:	amy.potter@mocha.com
Subject:	My Christmas list

☒ Save copy of outgoing message to sent folder Greeting cards

Dear Santa,

Please could I have the following things for Christmas:

Secret message

There might also be a space labelled 'Bcc' or 'blind copy'. It lets you send a copy to someone else without the person in the 'To' space knowing about it. Imagine that you know Ted really wants to go to Brad's house when Brad's sister is not in. You might send his sister an e-mail asking her to a movie and put Ted's e-mail address in the 'Blind copy' space so that he knows when she will be out. She won't know he's got the message, so she won't know he's avoiding her.

Message shorthand

Now type your message. It can be as long or as short as you like. If you're feeling really geeky, use some of these abbreviations:

BCNU   Be Seeing You

BTW   By The Way

CUL8R   See You Later

(For more abbreviations and net slang go to page 58.)

TFS – time for soccer!

It's in the mail!

When you've said all you need to say, click the 'Send' button and your message is off, whizzing down the phone line and off to find your friend's computer.

If you're using e-mail on a web page, the message is sent as soon as you click. If you're using an e-mail program on your computer, it will only go immediately if you're connected to the Internet. You don't need to be connected to write your messages, so you could write lots and then go on-line just to send them (it's cheaper that way as you don't stay on the phone for so long).

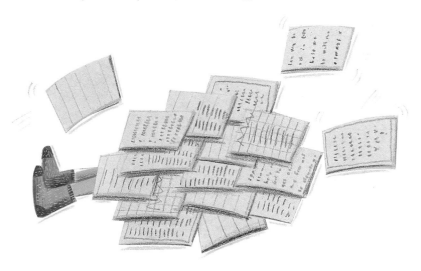

All your messages pile up in the 'Outbox' until you send them. It's like mailing letters in a mail box — they stay in the box until the postal worker comes and takes them out. If you don't connect and click 'Send and Receive', they will just stay there and no one will ever see them.

Anybody there?

It should take only a few seconds for your e-mail to get where it's going, but things don't always work quite like they should and sometimes a message gets delayed. So if you don't get a reply immediately, it doesn't mean nobody loves you any more.

Remember, too, that your friends won't get their e-mail until they log on to the Internet and check.

You got mail!

And what do you do when you get a message?

If you're using an e-mail program, the e-mail may be sent straight to your computer when you log on or you may have to pick it up. There will be a 'Send and Receive' or 'Check Mail' button.

If you're using e-mail on the Web, go to the web page and look for a note of how many messages you have or a button to click to 'Check Messages' or 'Check Inbox'.

Your inbox will look something like this:

	Check other mail | Empty trash			Showing 1-10 of 25 | next | last
View	checked mail		Choose folder	Delete
	Sender	Date	Size	Subject
☐	Eric Blair	Sun 19/12	859b	Mac ftp
☐	Anne Rooney	Sun 10/12	8k 📎	Kite flying - here's a picture!
☐	Anne Rooney	Sun 10/12	2k	Kite flying contest
☐	S.Pancho	Fri 08/12	1k	Free on Friday?
☐	Warner Village Cinema	Thur 07/12	3k	Performance information for Fri 08/12/01 – Thurs 14/12/01
☐	Bill Thompson	Fri 24/11	2k	Football fun

To read a message, click on either the subject, the name of the sender or a 'View' or 'Read' button. This opens the message for you to read. It will look at bit like this:

From:	Tod Potter
Date:	10 December 2001 13:14
To:	lauren@woppa2000.com
Subject:	Dan's party

Hiya
Are you going to Dan's party on Sat? If so, could your mom
please give me a lift :–) My dad's working late shift.

Thanks
Tod

Return to sender

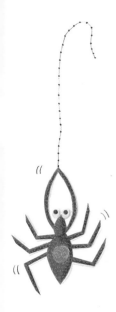

Sometimes, your message won't get through to where it's going. This might be because you made a mistake in the e-mail address or because the computer that handles your friend's mail isn't working (that's the e-mail provider's server, not your friend's computer, so don't alarm them by turning up with your tool kit). If they have a web e-mail account, it might be because they've got so many messages that their inbox is full to overflowing and it just can't take any more.

Bouncing back to you

If a message can't get through it is 'bounced' — sent back to you, usually with a subject line like 'Delivery failure' and a 'from' name like 'Mailer demon'.

Sounds nasty

There are some evil-sounding things you might come across as you dabble with e-mail:

● A demon is a program on a server that runs all the time, waiting for something to do, like handling e-mail or sending out a web page you've asked for.

● Demon is an internet service provider and you might see it in people's e-mail addresses, like this: susanne_the_zombie@zombies_r_us.demon.com

● A gremlin is what you blame if things keep going wrong with your computer. There isn't really any such thing, but it's nice to have something to blame!

I'LL GET BACK TO YOU

You've sent a message and got a reply — this could be the start of a wonderful e-friendship. Keep it going!

You can learn

- to reply to a message
- to send a message on to someone else
- to print or save a message
- to find more friends to e-mail

What now?

If you've had a reply to your message, you know the system works, so start using it! You might need to send a reply to the reply, you might want to let someone else know what's been said or you might want to keep a copy of the reply — even print it out and frame it as the first e-mail you ever got!

You said...

The screen showing a message you've got will have a 'Reply' button on it. Click this to start a message back to the same person. This saves you a bit of aggrevation, as the name and e-mail address will be filled in already. The subject will be filled in but with 'Re:' in front of whatever they had put.

'Re:' in e-mail means 'about' — it's from the Latin *res*, meaning 'thing', so 'Re:' is 'Thing we're talking about:'.

Usually, all the words of the original message to you are copied into the new message, but you might have the choice of starting with a blank screen.

Rub it out

If the text is all there and you don't want it, you can delete all of it. Click in the message, press the keys 'Ctrl' and 'A' (if you're using a PC) or ' ' (Option) and 'A' (if you're using a Mac) to select all the text and then 'Ctrl X' or 'Option X' to delete it.

If the message is there, there's often a way of telling which are the old bits and which are new. The old lines might all start with '>' or might be in a different color or style of text. Often, you'll want to reply to some of the points in the message. Click where you want to add an answer, press 'Enter' to start a new line and type your response.

From:	Lauren Sumner-Rooney
Date:	10 December 2001 13:22
To:	Tod Potter
Subject:	Re: Dan's party

Yes, sure. We'll pick you up at 7. What are you getting him?
I've got a really awesome scooter bag – you'll love it!
Seeya!
Lauren

-------Original Message-------
From: Tod Potter<todpotter@yahoo.com >
To: <lauren@woppa2000.com>
Sent: Sunday, December 10, 2001 1:14 pm
Subject: Dan's party

>Hiya
>Are you going to Dan's party on Sat? If so, could your

If there's lots of things you aren't answering, it's polite to delete them. To delete something, select it by dragging over it and then use 'Ctrl X' or 'Option X' to remove it.

Add any extras you want at the top or bottom and when you've finished, click 'Send' and you're done.

Help box

You can use these keyboard shortcuts to rub out, copy and stick things in your messages:

• 'Ctrl X' or 'Option X' to delete the item you've selected.

• 'Ctrl C' or 'Option C' to copy an item into the computer's memory ready to put in somewhere else.

• 'Ctrl V' or 'Option V' to paste in something you've copied or deleted.

You can use these keys with other pieces of writing too, not just your e-mail. So you can copy something out of a story you've written with a word-processor or pieces out of your e-mail into something else.

And she said...

What if you get some really juicy gossip that you've just got to pass on? You don't need to type it all in again, you can just send the message on to someone else.

...go forward!

On the screen showing the message, find the button marked 'Forward' but don't click yet! Some e-mail pages let you choose whether you want to send the message on as an 'attachment' or as 'in-line text'. An attachment is an extra, separate piece you send with a message. You'll find out more about that in 'Attaching stuff' on page 38. 'In-line text' means the words in the original message are copied straight into your new e-mail. That's the one you want. Now you can click 'Forward'.

A new message starts, with the subject line filled in and probably with 'FW:' in front of the subject. This stands for 'Forwarded'. All the original message will be there, including a line that tells you who sent it originally. Again, you can take pieces out and add more words of your own. Don't forget to fill in the 'To:' space with the e-mail address of the person you want to send it on to or it won't know where to go. When you've finished, click 'Send' and off it goes.

From:	lauren@woppa2ooo.com (lauren's mail)
To:	Anne Rooney
Cc:	
Bcc:	
Subject:	FW: Dan's party

I got this from Tod. We're giving him a lift to the party. Do you want one as well?

L xx

------- Original Message -------

From: Tod Potter<todpotter@yahoo.com>

To: <lauren@woppa2ooo.com>

Subject: Dan's party

I've got proof!

E-mail is half way between a phone call and a letter. Unless you print your e-mail out or save it on your computer, it's gone when you're not on-line, just like a phone call. If you're using an e-mail program like Outlook Express, there will be a copy of the messages you receive and send on your computer, but if you're using web e-mail you won't have a copy unless you specifically save it or download it. If you think there might be a fight about who said what, it's worth doing that.

Down the load

If you're using web e-mail look for a button or menu option to save the message or download it. Downloading means copying it from the computer your e-mail's stored on (the server) and saving it on to your own. Uploading means copying stuff from your computer on to a server.

'Offloading' means getting someone else to do things you're supposed to be doing — like offloading the dishes on to your brother!

Hard copy

Once you've got a copy, you can print it out.
If you print it from the web page, you will probably only
get the piece of the message that you can see on screen.
Fine if that's all there is, but if it's a long message you
might miss the really important part. So you might want
to download it first or copy and paste the message into a
document on your computer. You can print copies of e-mail
you send, too. A good idea if you're promising anything!

Nobody loves me :-(

If you don't have enough people sending you e-mails,
find an e-mail pen pal. They can be anywhere in the
world, but it still takes only seconds or minutes for your
messages to go backwards and forwards. (But remember
they might be asleep when you send your message —
allow for different time zones.)

Go to
http://www.bigfishonline.co.uk/whizzkids
to find links to web pages that can help you
to find an e-mail pen pal.

ATTACHING STUFF

When you write to someone, you can put just the letter in the envelope or you can stick in some other things, too, like a picture or story. You can do just the same with e-mail. Things that you send with your e-mail are called 'attachments'.

You can learn

- how to add a picture or story to send with your message
- which file formats to use for your attachments
- what to do with an attachment you get from someone else

Form an attachment

You can't always say all you want in an e-mail. It's usually just plain text – boring old black without any styling or pictures – and that might not be enough. If you want to send something else – pictures you've drawn, a story you've written, photos you've taken or maybe a map of how to get to your party – you don't have to use snail-mail instead. You can add an attachment to your e-mail that will be sent along with it.

Look at this!

OK, you can't send one of your baseball cards or the sock your friend left behind when you had a sleep-over – but you can send a piece of music or voice mail, a cartoon or even a little bit of multimedia you've put together in your spare time.

I wish I could attach him to an e-mail!

Stretching the envelope

To send an attachment, find a button labelled something like 'Attach file' or 'Enclosure' in your e-mail program or web page. Click on this and it will open a dialogue box for you to show which file you want to attach. You might need to move through the folders on your hard disk to find it.

Click 'Attach' or 'OK'. And then when you send your e-mail, the attachment is sent too – just like stuffing more things in the envelope.

File formats

If you're going to send stuff to a pal, check they can use it when it gets there! Computer programs organize information in different ways and some of the ways can only be understood by the same program. If you want to send a story you've written in Word, check that your friend has Word. If not, you'll need to save the story in a different way that they can use. Choose 'Save as' from the file menu when you save your work and look through the file format options. Here are some tips on the best formats to use for:

Stories and other writing: look for an option to save as 'plain text' or '.txt' or 'ASCII'. You won't get the text styles and colors and pictures you've used, but the words will all get through.

Pictures: the best choices are '.gif' or 'jpeg' ('.jpg'). These are the picture formats used for the World Wide Web, and so anyone with a web browser can look at them. If you can't save your pictures in one of these formats, use '.bmp' (which stands for bitmap) which you can open in any painting program. But look out – a '.bmp' file can be very big (take up a lot of computer memory and disk space) and that means it will take a long time to send.

Spreadsheets and databases: you might not send these very often, but if it's part of your homework, the catalogue of your DVD collection or the spreadsheet that shows how long it will take you to pay for a scooter, save it as a 'comma separated value' or '.csv' file if your friends don't have the same program as you.

Sounds: if you're sending music or voice clips, look for an option to save as '.wav', 'MIDI' ('.mid') or 'MP3'.

Video and animation: getting to serious stuff now – these are going to be big, so check out 'Zip it up!' on page 42. Look for 'mpeg' ('.mpg'), '.avi' or '.gif' ('multigif' or 'animated gif').

Zip it up!

If you want to send a large file – one that shows a file size over 400K (kilobytes) or so – remember that it will go slowly. It will cost you more in phone time to send it and your friend more to download it. And if it's 1MB (1,024 kilobytes) or so, it may be too big to send by e-mail at all. That doesn't mean you can't send it, but that you need to zip, or compress, it first. This takes out all the unnecessary parts to make the file smaller. Your friend needs to unzip, or decompress, it afterwards, and that puts all the bits back in. Think of it as sending a beach ball in the mail – you wouldn't send it inflated, you'd let it down and let your friend blow it up again when it got there.

> There's not much bounce in this ball!

 You'll need some software to compress your files. There is some you can try out for free; check out: **http://www.bigfishonline.co.uk/whizzkids** to find links to some.

Enclosure

What if someone sends you an attachment? You'll be able to see if there's an attachment with a message because it will have a little picture – called an icon – beside it. This usually shows a paperclip.

📎	✉ Anne Clark	Re: My holiday pictures

Save it

If you're using an e-mail program, the e-mail has already been downloaded to your computer, so you just need to save the attachment somewhere and look at it. There will be an option in the menus or a button to 'Save attachment'. Click this and choose where you want to put it. You can then open it using a suitable program.

Detach an attachment

If you're using e-mail on the Web, you might be able to look at the attachment without downloading it or you may have to download it to your own computer first. It will depend on the file format of the attachment and the e-mail page. If it's a picture in a form that can be displayed on a web page (a 'gif' or 'jpeg') you can probably look at it without downloading it. If it's something the browser can't deal with, you'll need to download it first. There will be a button to do this. Click on it and choose where you want to save the file on your disk. If the file is large, it will take a while to download. But you can go away and do other stuff while it's doing it.

Unzip it!

If you get a zipped or compressed file, you'll need to unzip, or decompress, it before you can look at it. You will certainly need to download it before you can do anything with it. You'll need the right piece of software to reinflate the beach ball. If you're using a PC, it's likely to be a '.zip' file. Use something like Winzip to unzip it. If you're using a Mac, it's most likely to have been 'stuffed' using StuffIt.

 There are links on
http://www.bigfishonline.co.uk/whizzkids
to get the right piece software to decompress
your attachments.

If you haven't got the same type of computer or compression software as the person who sent you the attachment, you might be in trouble. Check with them first what you can both handle.

YOU CAN MANAGE!

Save time and hassle by keeping track of your mail and building an address book for all your e-mail contacts.

You can learn

- to keep an address book of e-mail addresses
- to sort out your sent mail and messages you get
- to clean your room! Just kidding — to keep your mail box clean so there's room for new messages

Address book

A-Z of e-mail addresses

Bet you can't remember zipcodes of more than a few people? Most of us can't. And chances are, you won't be able to remember loads of e-mail addresses either. Lots of '@yahoo's and '@postmark's aren't easy to keep sorted unless you've got a really sharp brain — and who wants to be like that? So it makes sense to build an address book on the computer.

Keep your precious brain cells for important stuff like sports scores!

Addressing it

Whatever service or program you use for your e-mail, there will be something you can click on to look at and add to an address book. This lets you type in — or copy from been sent — the names and e-mail addresses of the people you want to keep in touch with. Then, when you want to send an e-mail, you look for the name of the person, click to send them a message and all the goobledegook of their e-mail address appears like magic in the 'To' space with no mistakes.

Address book

Do it now!

Start now by typing in the names and e-mail addresses of the people you e-mail most often. If you get into the habit of adding new e-mail addresses as soon as you know them or use them, you'll soon have a really useful address book and you'll hardly ever need to type an e-mail address again.

You can usually set a 'nickname' or 'alias' for someone in your address book – like 'Dad' or 'Wild Pig'. Then you can pick this from the list to use their e-mail address. (But don't use 'Worst enemy' or 'Dan's stupid friend I met at Christmas' as they might be upset if they see it in the header to their e-mail.)

No mess

If you're using something like Outlook Express, you can store loads of other details, too, like phone numbers and snail-mail addresses. Then you can keep your whole address book on the computer. It's neater than a book full of crossed out old addresses and changed phone numbers because you can update it without making a mess.

Not wanted

You might be able to set your e-mail so that any address you reply to is automatically copied into your address book. This is pretty handy, but make sure you check now and then that it doesn't get full of addresses you don't really want. You can get rid of them by clicking on them and on a 'Delete' or trash can button.

Boxes and folders

The e-mail system you use will sort messages you write into an 'Out' folder, 'Outbox' or folder of 'Sent' mail and messages you get into an 'Inbox' or 'In' folder. After that, it's up to you to organize your messages more carefully.

If there are lots of messages you want to keep, it's worth creating folders for them and moving them into the right places regularly. You might have a folder called 'School' for messages about homework and one called 'Friends' for fun messages.

Look at the buttons or menus on your e-mail page or program to find out how to create folders. You can usually just drag the icon for a message into a folder to move it. Keeping your messages organized makes it much easier when you want to find something later.

Waste of space

Have you got a pile of comics three years old under your bed? If so, you'll probably fill up your computer or mail folder with a lot of e-mails you don't really need. If there's something you aren't going to need again, throw it away! If it's stored on your own computer, it's wasting your disk space. And if you use a web e-mail service, when your space is full you won't be able to get any more messages.

Trash it!

To get rid of messages you don't need any more, click on the message or its icon and then on a 'Delete' or trash can button. Often, this isn't enough to get rid of it for good. Think about it — if you don't empty the trash in your room, what happens? It just fills up! The same is true of the trash can on the computer or e-mail page. Unless you choose to empty it, the stuff stays there — so you still haven't got any more space. Throw the things away that you don't want and then make sure you empty the trash can.

E-MAIL WHIZZ

You now know pretty
much all there is to
know about e-mail,
so time to fast-track to
the really cool stuff.

You can learn

- to get e-mail sent to you on topics you're interested in
- to send e-mail to famous people
- to get yourself heard
- to avoid chains, spam and flames!
- to change your signature
- to add art to your messages

Get more mail

You don't need to depend on your friends
to send you interesting mail — which is
probably a good thing. You can join a
newsgroup and get sent regular news or updates
on a topic that interests you. There are thousands of
newsgroups, covering all kinds of topics from sports
to keeping stick insects, animal charities to local info,
fan clubs to movie-news updates.

Interested party

In newsgroups, all the info comes from other people interested in the topic. They send in an e-mail, and everyone who's said they want to join gets sent the message. It's a great way to get answers to questions on a topic as all the people reading are keen, too.

There are links on
http://www.bigfishonline.co.uk/whizzkids
to help you find a newsgroup you'll like.

It's considered rude to send things that are 'off topic' — unrelated to the interests of the group — or to use a newsgroup for advertising. It's best to watch what comes through for a while until you've got the hang of it.

What do you do if you see a spaceman? Park in it, man.

Teehee mail!

Get a joke sent to you each morning to brighten your day! There are lots of websites and services that will send you e-mail messages if you ask — anything from jokes and sports scores to details of the films coming up at your local cinema and reminders of when your library books are due back.

You don't know me, but...

Ever wanted to talk to your favorite band or the president? You can do it by e-mail!

Lots of famous people have an e-mail address on their website. There's usually a link so you click on it and a box pops up for you to type in your message. Some famous people get hundreds of e-mails a day, so you might need to wait to get a reply. But you usually will get one; they wouldn't give an e-mail address if they didn't want you to write.

Have a voice

You can use e-mail to get your voice heard on serious issues, too. You might be able to appeal against local plans — to put a road through a meadow, for instance — or sign a petition. And no one can tell from your e-mail address you're a kid, so it's a great way of being taken seriously.

Eeek!

Chain mail

Sooner or later, you'll get sent e-mail that's part of a chain. It might be trying to persuade you to buy something, to send money or it might just be for fun — jokes or a funny story.

You don't have to pass it on and you certainly shouldn't send any money. If there are nasty threats in the mail that you will have bad luck if you don't pass it on, ignore them. It's total garbage. If it's just jokes or something else harmless and fun, pass it on if you want, but remember you don't have to.

No more flaming spam!

'Flaming' is sending an unpleasant e-mail about someone, usually to lots of people at once. It sometimes happens to people who send inappropriate messages to a newsgroup — so be careful.

Spam is junk mail sent by e-mail. The chain mail I've just mentioned is an example. More often, it's advertising material. Usually it's harmless but boring info about stuff you aren't interested in, but some of it is for unpleasant websites. Don't follow the links, just delete the mail. If it upsets you, tell a grown-up. You can change your e-mail address easily if it becomes a problem.

No hassle

If you've chosen an e-mail account that's intended for children and you get e-mails advertising nasty stuff, tell the people running the web page you used — there will be an address to contact the site. They should be able to filter out messages from that source in future so that you aren't hassled.

Spam was originally a meat product invented during World War II. Junk e-mail is called spam after a sketch in a comedy program called 'Monty Python' in the 970s. It was about a café that sold 'Spam, tomato and Spam, egg and Spam, egg, bacon and Spam...'!

And finally...

At the end of your message, your mail program or the web page you're using will probably add a bit of text, called a 'signature'. If it's a free e-mail service, it will probably be a plug for their e-mail service. Something like 'Get a free e-mail account with mye-mail.com' and a link to their website.

You can probably change the signature to something a bit cooler. If you're using an e-mail program, you can certainly do this. Look for an option on the web page or in the menus for your mail program.

ASCII art

Before computers were good at doing pictures, people used to make up little pictures using text. It's a development of smileys (see page 60). You do it by typing letters and spaces to make a pattern.

You can put a bit of ASCII art, or art made of typed symbols, in your signature — remember that you won't need to type it in every time if you've set it up to be your signature, it will be added automatically. So it's worth spending a bit of time working out what you want. And you can change your signature whenever you get bored. How about a witch or a cat for Halloween?

```
     o
    oo
   oooo
 oooooooo
  | * * |
   \ ~ /
     v
```

```
                         ) )
  /\_/\              ( (
 ( o o )               ) )
  ≤ ~ ≥ ~ ~ ~ ~ ~ )
 (                        )
 | | ~ ~ ~ ~ ~ / /
 d |              c_/
```

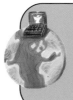

If you're not very artistic, find ASCII art on the Web and copy it into your signature. There are links to some from
http://www.bigfishonline.co.uk/whizzkids

LEARN THE LINGO

In e-mail you don't need to follow the spelling and punctuation rules you learn at school — e-mail has its own rules (or non-rules). You can use spelling, spacing and punctuation to get across a way of speaking, such as s-l-o-w-i-n-g d-o-w-n or SHOUTING. If something is reeeeaaaallly coooool, you can spell it in a drawl. And you don't have to uSe capITalS in the usUAl waY. You can use slang spellings — like 'kewl' — and check out an on-line dictionary of net slang for special words only used in e-mail and newsgroups. Here are some more abbreviations and check out the smileys on pages 60–61.

ATM	At The Moment
AWHFY	Are We Having Fun Yet?
BAC	By Any Chance
B/C	Because
BIC	Best In Class
BION	Believe It Or Not
BRB	Be Right Back
BTDT	Been There, Done That
DYOH	Do Your Own Homework
EM	E-mail Me
EOD	End Of Discussion
ETA	Estimated Time of Arrival
F2F	Face To Face

F2T	(Are you) Free To Talk?
FYA	For Your Amusement
FYI	For Your Information
G2G	Gotta go
GGN	Gotta Go Now
GOOML	Get Out Of My Life
HAK	Hugs and Kisses
HAND	Have A Nice Day
HHOK	Ha Ha Only Kidding
JAM	Just A Moment
JK	Just Kidding
LJBF	Let's Just Be Friends
LMA	Leave Me Alone
LOL	Lots Of Love
NAGI	Not A Good Idea
ONNA	Oh No, Not Again!
OTT	Over The Top
PAW	Parents Are Watching
RNA	Rang, No Answer
RUOK	Are you OK?
SRY	Sorry
SU	Shut Up
SUNOILTY	Shut Up, No One Is Listening To You
TC	Take Care
THO	Though
TTFN	Ta Ta For Now
W4ME@	Wait For Me At
W8	Wait
WFM	Works For Me
W/O	Without
WOT	Waste Of Time
YANETUT	You Are Not Expected To Understand This

SMILEYS :-)

It's sometimes hard to get across how you're feeling in an e-mail, but it's easy to give the wrong impression. Use smileys to make sure you get it right.

:-)	happy
:-(	sad
;-)	winking
:-=)	face with mustache
:-P	sticking tongue out
:-x	kissing
{:-)	with hairstyle
B-)	with shades/goggles
8:-)	with glasses on forehead
I-)	asleep
I-O	asleep and snoring/yawning
:-e	disappointed

(: +(scared

+:-)   priest

@;-)   a flirt

#-(been partying all night

=:-)   with bangs/sticky-up hair

? :-)   with curls

:,-(crying

: - D   laughing

:-| 'have an ordinary day'

. -)   one eye

<:-)   dunce

(: -)   egghead

@:-)   with cool hat

USEFUL WORDS

address
Where someone's e-mail must be sent to for them to get it. An e-mail address is usually made up of a name, the @ (at) symbol, the name of an e-mail service provider, such as yahoo, and then '.com', '.com' or '.net'.

alias
A short name you can pick to call up someone's e-mail address.

attachment
Extra file that you send along with e-mail. It might be a picture or a piece of music, for example.

blind copy or 'Bcc'
Send a 'blind copy' of an e-mail to an address in this space. The person in the 'To' space won't know the copy has been sent.

bounced
E-mail sent back to the sender because it can't be delivered.

Copy or 'Cc'
Send a copy of an e-mail to the e-mail address in this space.

delete
Permanently remove something, such as text in a message or a message from your e-mail box.

demon
Computer program that runs all the time, waiting to carry out its particular activity, like passing on e-mail to another computer.

download
Copy information from a computer on the World Wide Web on to your own computer.

e-mail
Electronic mail. This allows you to send messages, and often also pictures and other information, to anyone else who has an e-mail address. The information is sent over the Internet.

enclosure see **attachment**

file format
The way information is stored so that a particular type of computer program can understand it.

flame
Send a nasty e-mail about someone to lots of other people.

inbox
The folder where all the e-mail messages you get are kept.

Internet
A worldwide network of linked computers.

Internet Service Provider (ISP)
A company that provides you with a connection to the Internet.

mailer demon
A program that runs all the time, waiting to work with any e-mail sent out or coming in.

modem
Equipment that allows your computer to be connected to the Internet. It converts information from the form your computer can understand to the form it needs to be in to travel down the phone line and on to the Internet.

newsgroup
A group you can join to be sent e-mails about a particular topic. Any messages you send to the newsgroup are sent on to everyone else on the list.

off-line
Not connected to the Internet.

on-line
Connected to the Internet.

outbox
The folder where e-mail messages you have written are kept until they are sent.

password
Secret word used to identify you when you want to look at or send your e-mail.

paste
Add words to your message that you have copied or removed from somewhere else.

server
A computer that provides a service for other computers, such as providing web pages that have been asked for.

smiley
Set of characters arranged to look like a face and used to get across feelings or attitudes.

snail-mail
The ordinary postal service.

spam
Unwanted, junk e-mail.

upload
Copy information from your own computer on to a computer on the Internet.

web browser
Computer program that lets you use the World Wide Web.

World Wide Web
Over a billion linked 'pages' of information in a format that you can look at if you are on the Internet and have a web browser.

zip
To make a computer file take up less disk space.

INDEX